To my love
of many years,
and of many years
to come.

Library of Congress Cataloging-in-Publication Data
Hanson, Warren.
Older love / by Warren Hanson.
   p.   cm.
isbn 0-931674-40-9 (hc. : alk. paper)
1. Married people--Poetry. 2. Love poetry, American.
1. Title.
PS3558.A54378O43 1999
811'.54--dc21   99-19826

Waldman House Press, Inc.
525 North 3rd Street
Minneapolis, Minnesota 55401

OLDER LOVE

Warren Hanson

Waldman House Press, Inc.

Young love is magic!

Bright!

Electric!

Lightning! Sparks! and Fire!

Burning with new passion

and the hot flame of desire.

But when that fire grows quiet,

there remains the radiance of

a romance that goes on growing

in the glow of older love.

Older love has magic too,

and myth, and mystery,

as two souls become one spirit,

with one heart, one history.

It's the miracle that turns a common promise into gold.

The lyrical duet of two new lovers growing old.

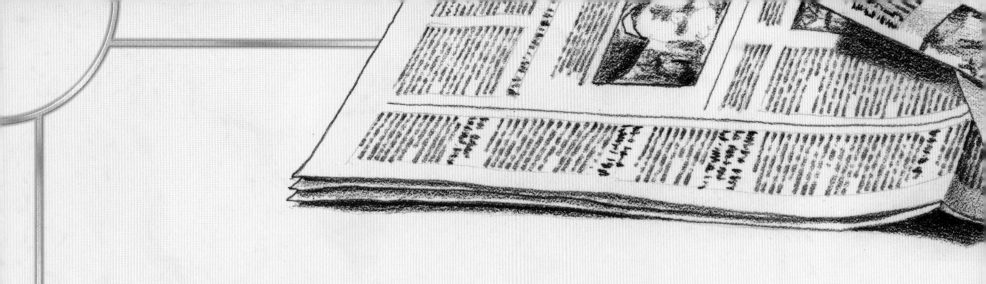

We hear this old love every day, in ways we'd never think.

The gentle plink of dishes swishing in the kitchen sink.

The sound of slippered footsteps
in the hallway overhead,

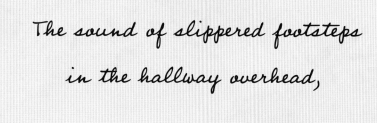

when I have risen early,

and you have stayed in bed.

The morning paper.

Coffee in the same old favorite cups.

The fond, familiar rituals

that nothing interrupts.

The joyful jingle of your keys.

Your telephone hello.

The quiet, happy humming of that song from long ago.

Older love still dances when they play that favorite song.

It reminds us of romances that would last all summer long.

Those songs of summer days are fading into memory,

but that romance will last forever.

Golden oldies.

You and me.

MEET
THE B
The First Album

There's a nice, familiar comfort in a love that isn't new,

that has had some bumps and bruises, and been scuffed a time or two.

It's a love you can relax in. It is casual and loose,

with that soft and supple fit you get from years of loving use.

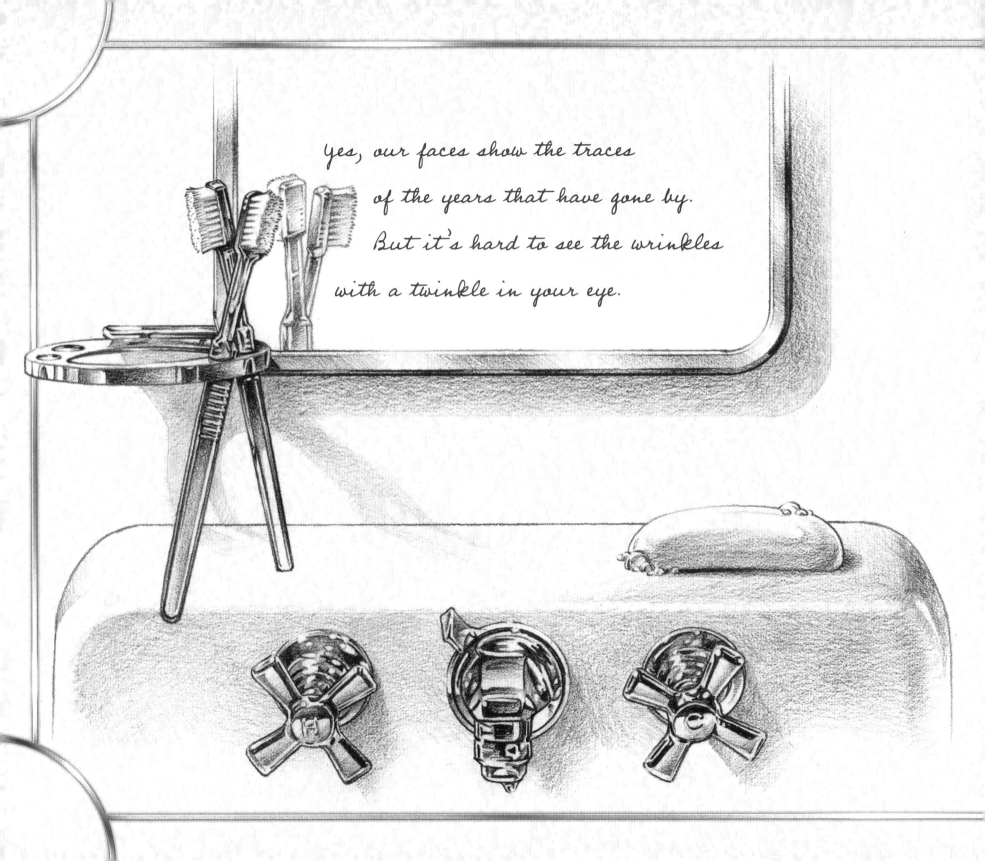

Yes, our faces show the traces
of the years that have gone by.
But it's hard to see the wrinkles
with a twinkle in your eye.

And though the vision may have softened,

one thing still is crystal clear —

older love looks so much better

when you hold it very near.

If this old love doesn't tingle with every single touch,

it doesn't mean that we don't love each other quite as much.

In fact, in our maturity, our love can still increase

in its sweetness and security, its power and its peace.

So, though a touch may not send shivers, it delivers so much more.

In these hands we hold our older love, and that's what hands are for.

They are hands that cradled babies, giving comfort in the night.

Hands to guide the growing, and to point out what is right.

Hands to tickle tummies,

and to wipe away the tears.

They are hands that hold each other,

as they have... and will... for years.

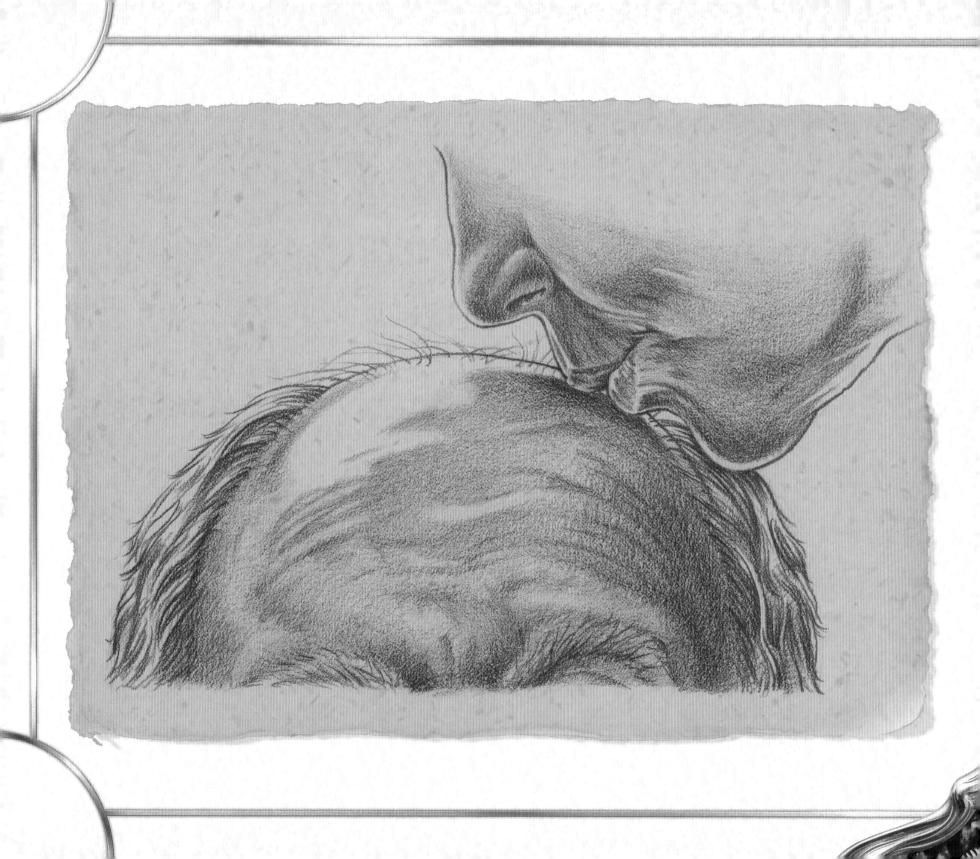

Then, as the gleam of purest silver starts to sparkle in our hair,

every strand becomes more precious,

as the hair becomes more rare!

And the beauty of our bodies is retreating with our youth.

But older love sees beauty more in honesty and truth.

The truth is, we're not perfect.

We're not beautiful or young.

Our thrills are mostly wilted, and our springs are mostly sprung.

But...

...we are perfect... for each other.

Me for you and you for me.

Older love holds us together.
Bound forever. Perfectly.

Older love is poured out slowly,

and is savored by the sip.

It has color, and aroma,

and is sweet upon the lip.

If it is aged with gentle patience,

the reward is worth the wait,

and the world will spin with vintage love.

A love to celebrate!

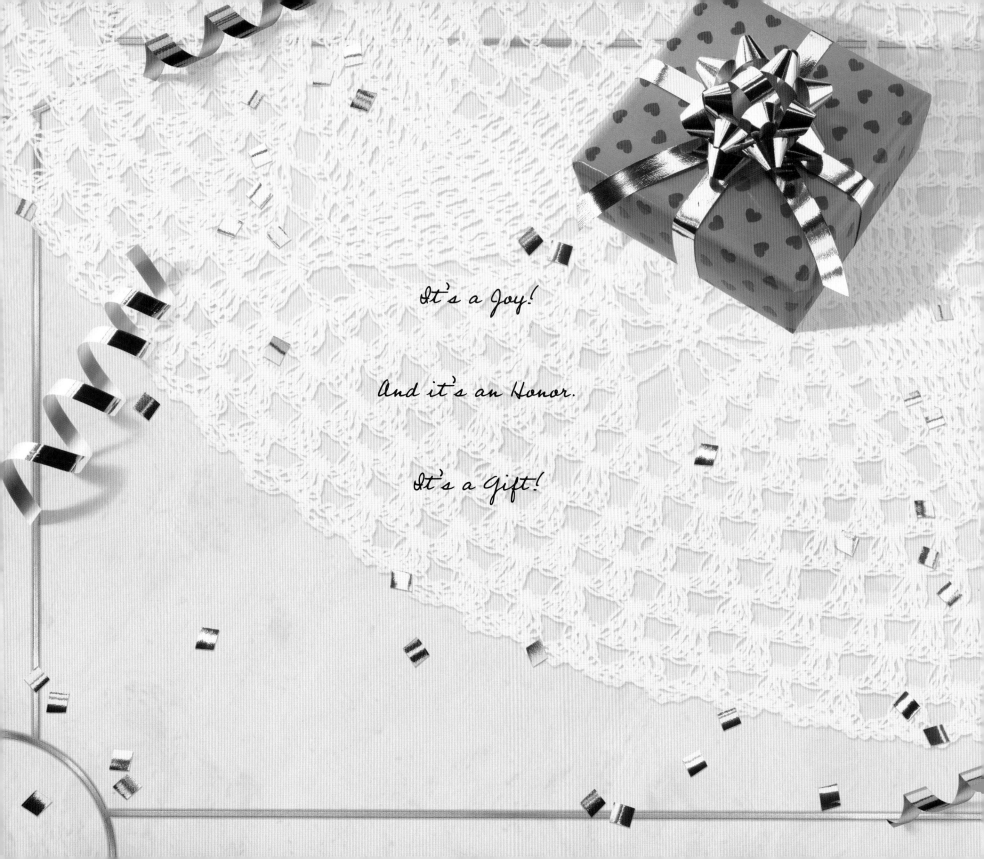

It's a Joy!

And it's an Honor.

It's a Gift!

And it's a Vow

to be good to one another,

both forever

and for now.

It's the duty of confessing

that I fail you every day.

It's the beauty and the blessing

that you love me anyway.

It's forgiving, and forgetting.

And remembering.

And then...

it is knowing that I'm going to make

the same mistakes again.

Just two ordinary people,
that is all we'll ever be,
with an everyday devotion
to each other, you and me.

Yet our ordinary evenings
bring extraordinary calm,
as we share the still tranquility,
as sacred as a psalm.

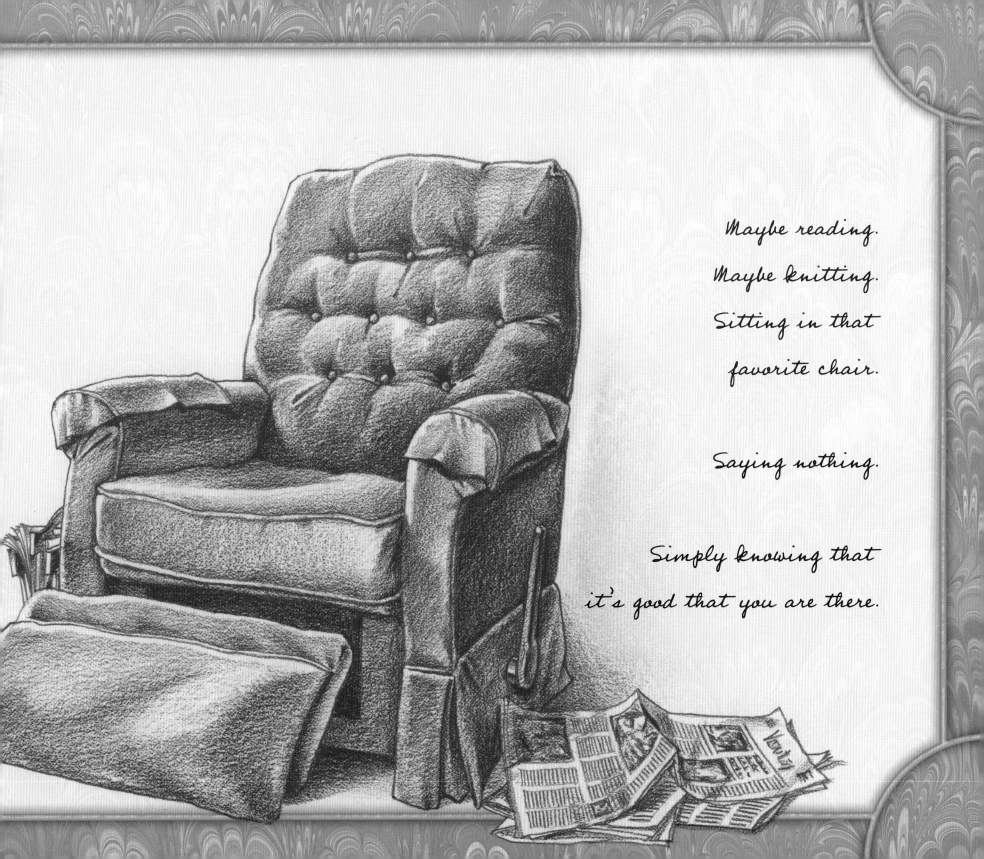

Maybe reading.
Maybe knitting.
Sitting in that
favorite chair.

Saying nothing.

Simply knowing that
it's good that you are there.

And when the day is over and we settle into bed,

we each start to read a book, but end up nodding off instead.

That book will wait 'til later, for another rendezvous.

And yet, between those covers is a fairy tale come true.

It's an old familiar story, and we both know how it ends,

as the passionate young lovers become passionate old friends.

Older love is hands and hearts and souls as they unite

every morning, every evening,

every day and every night.

Like the sun and moon and stars that light the heavens up above,

these two lives will shine together,

with the glow of older love.